"This is one of the most value-packed b̶ a long
time. If you're looking for ⌐ seful
tips and help harness ance
t̶

— TAREK FAD
Nomura Ass ...te East

"There is an impressive wealth of information in
The Art of Executive Appearance. I'm always in the spotlight, and
this is an effective way to brush up on fundamentals and learn
a few insider tricks. It will change your perception on what you
think is possible."

— LENA KOMILEVA FLOYD, Chief Economist,
Director at G+ Economics

"In a time of growing media convergence around
the world, a solid foundation of camera appearance
skills is vitally important. With refreshing brevity
and clarity, *The Art of Executive Appearance* is bound to become
required reading."

— HUSSEIN AMIN, Professor of Journalism
and Mass Communication, American University in Cairo

"As TV pundits multiply across media channels and anchors
compete for your attention, it's more crucial than ever to stand
out...for the right reasons. Yousef's book is a useful and enjoyable
guide to effectively send your message across the crowded
airwaves, while looking great doing it."

— ASHRAF LAIDI, CEO, Intermarket Strategy Ltd and Author of
"Currency Trading and Intermarket Analysis"

*"You act like mortals
in all that you fear,
and like immortals
in all that you desire."*

—LUCIUS ANNAEUS SENECA,
On the Shortness of Life

THE **ART** OF EXECUTIVE APPEARANCE

5 SIMPLE WAYS TO IMPRESS ON CAMERA AND **INSPIRE A TELEVISION AUDIENCE**

THIRD EDITION

YOUSEF GAMAL EL-DIN

Table of Contents

Introduction

The thick, soundproofed doors of the television studio swing open for you, and as you step toward the set, the chilled air and the sweltering lights stop you in your tracks. Your breathing gets heavier, your heart is pounding out of your chest, and the infamous butterflies begin twirling in your gut.

"This is it."

That's when frenzied thoughts start spinning in your head: *"What will they think of me? Is my sweat already showing? Should I have worn that other shirt? Why did my hairdresser have to go on holiday this week? Will I make the most of this opportunity to tell my story?"*

You are not alone with these questions. I'll put my hand up and admit that those are thoughts I've wrestled with too. We are innately social creatures, and the prospect of "putting ourselves out there" can be terrifying. Self-conscious behavior is hard-wired to our desire for group belonging, and a media appearance has the power to stir in us a set of complex emotions. We dread ridicule and shame. After all, the smallest mistakes can translate into online blooper videos gone viral.

Here's an exercise for you: When was the last time you saw someone on TV or *YouTube* and made a judgment before you even listened to what they had to say? Your verdict often comes as swiftly as flipping the channel or closing a tab in your browser.

"This guy's shirt is so nineties. I'm not in the mood for a history lesson." CLICK.

Most people claim to be nonjudgmental, yet communication studies demonstrate that your appearance often matters far more than anything you might say.

"That's a really colorful scarf. Definitely a bit over-the-top. Not something I want to watch right now." CLICK.

Or, *"I'm sorry, but I can't take you seriously!"* CLICK.

When you step into the limelight, you enter a structured reality that is framed not by you, but by the media. Instead of experiencing an event firsthand, viewers are getting a broad version of reality through the prism of storytellers. And as a leading broadcaster, I guarantee you it's all about being aware, *being in tune*, with the fundamental routines of appearing on camera. The road to excellence is the same in any other art or science. There are shortcuts, yes, but there's no miraculous pill that has been invented (yet).

A victory in front of the camera can clear the thick fog that typically clouds unchartered frontiers. With the right media training, you can reach new heights in your business and personal life. The bell is ringing to think bigger.

Still, I see people venture out in front of the camera time and time again without giving serious thought to their appearance. They convince themselves that going on camera is not a big deal, or they believe that because they themselves are important, they don't need to put in any effort. That could not be further from the truth!

COMMON DELUSIONS ABOUT BEING ON-CAMERA

"I can wing it."
Sure you can, but just as with anything you "wing" in life, it may fly off in the completely wrong direction.

"People are not going to notice what I'm wearing."
Breaking news: of course they will notice. We are intuitively positioned to process first impressions. If that is your state of mind when you go on stage, then you'll underperform.

"The people in the TV studio know what they're doing. They will do all that's required for me to look my best right before I step on the set."
Reality check: not all television presenters and guests have a stylist or makeup artist at the scene.

"I'm not photogenic enough for a TV appearance."
Believe it or not, a statement like that is just your way for conveniently rationalizing your anxiety. When you believe that a variable like "photogenic" cannot be altered, then you can better deal with your do-nothing-about-it attitude.

"My voice sounds weird. I don't like the way I sound."
Listening to your voice while you talk and listening to yourself back in a recording are scientifically two different experiences. Has anybody ever told you that you sound "weird"? It's all in your mind!

Let's reset then. Take a deep breath. Clear your mind from these misleading beliefs.

Start with a clean slate and prepare to embrace a new approach for an effective on-air persona that will launch you toward realizing your goals.

Over the course of my eventful career in live television, including top news networks *Bloomberg Television* and *CNBC*, I had access to the world's most powerful people in business and politics. Some of the signature shows I anchored were *Bloomberg Markets* and *Capital Connection*, both live, daily programs that provide a bridge between the market action in Asia and the United States. The journey gave me insights into what makes a television appearance memorable. And now this is my chance to share those visions with you.

My objective in writing this concise handbook originated in my personal experience. Over the years, I had a front-row seat to witness some of the deepest fears that often limit clarity of thought for guests the moment we're live on-air. The weaknesses in hundreds of ambitious men and women from around the globe who had decided to go on camera struck me as nothing short of shocking.

Regardless of whether you are preparing for major appearances on leading TV news networks or experimenting with personal video content on *YouTube*, this guide to looking your very best will greatly amplify your message. I will dedicate the following pages to sharing with you the many trade secrets that I have amassed over my years in front of the camera.

Other sources provide perplexing material on how to handle the camera, information that is usually squeezed in as a small section in a larger, broader book. By contrast, *The Art of Executive Appearance* offers an entirely new level of razor-sharp tips for professionals on the move. It contains actionable information that people from all backgrounds can channel into easy-to-develop television habits.

A better understanding of how to engage on camera makes life easier for all stakeholders and, more importantly, keeps viewers focused on what you're saying.

My book is also an invaluable resource for those shaping content behind the camera, from leading prime-time producers to the folks who produce short corporate videos. Even public relations practitioners and official spokespeople can use this book to their advantage.

***The Art of Executive Appearance* serves as a trusted template for succeeding in front of the camera and inspiring audiences.** Now in its third edition, the book has matured through feedback from readers like you.

Here in these pages, I include solutions to issues that no other author has addressed.

Whether you like it or not, your public image is critical to you, the people you care about, and the future prospects of your business. By mastering my five routines for your executive appearance on television, you'll be able to readily capitalize on any publicity that comes your way. You'll learn about what I've coined the **OC-M-BC** process for short.

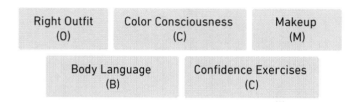

It covers everything from choosing the right outfit, to navigating body language and confidence exercises.

We have not met in person yet, but through the journey of this book, we'll be spending some time together. I am truly privileged to have the opportunity to be of service to you.

My blueprint will bring a valuable boost to your success. It has a proven record of making the kind of impact that transforms lives. And you'll enjoy the experience as well!

Here's to you looking great on camera.

Choose
the Right
Outfit (O)

0

Clothing is one of the bedrocks of a masterful appearance on camera. What you wear says a lot about you—that's why your intuitive aspiration is to look what you perceive as "good." At a basic level, this is influenced by your background plus the accepted social and fashion trends. The reason you picked up this book is for you to be convincing on television and get your message across to the people watching.

A bit of a caveat upfront: TV audiences have changed dramatically. We live in a time where attention is a scarce commodity. Recent research looked at a phenomenon known as second-screen viewing—that's the use of smartphones and tablets while watching television. To most people's surprise, they found lower news recall and comprehension rates. So much for our much-touted multitask abilities! [1]

That equates into a reduced chance of being listened to if you break it down for every second of airtime. Let's begin to tackle the challenge head-on by going through a few golden rules of attire, which we in the TV business live by. We'll then dive deeper into what are some suitable choices from your wardrobe.

Thanks to the complex biological mechanisms of our brains, your outfit can easily distract viewers. By all means be stylish, but if the message is what matters, your appearance needs to play a supportive role to your spoken words. Unless you are known for bold, extreme fashion statements like celebrity pop superstars Lady Gaga or Rihanna, don't go wild with your outfit.

For example, unless it's what your brand is about, don't show up in a tuxedo for a morning show at a time when everyone else is casually attired for a relaxed breakfast discussion. A tank top and tattered light blue jeans are equally unhelpful at a formal, televised debate among presidential candidates. And the same goes for a tailored and expensive suit if you're broadcasting from the Afghan capital of Kabul with gunfire in the background.

If you do adopt a radically contrarian fashion approach, the number of people listening attentively to what you're saying will take a dive. The average viewer (you and I included) has a finite capacity to process different stimuli simultaneously. When more space is taken up by appearance cues, less space will be available to filter your message.

ABC of Attire Decision-Making

W hat comes to mind when you reflect on a few of the greatest speeches of the twentieth century? What images and emotions surface when you recall former U.S. President John F. Kennedy's speech, "We choose to go to the Moon," or civil rights activist Martin Luther King Jr.'s "I have a Dream"?

Here's an emotional excerpt from the transcript of Kennedy's speech given at Houston's Rice Stadium in 1962: *"We choose to go to the moon. We choose to go to the moon in this decade and do the other things, not because they are easy, but because they are hard, because that goal will serve to organize and measure the best of our energies and skills, because that challenge is one that we are willing to accept, one we are unwilling to postpone, and one which we intend to win, and the others, too."* [2]

Even if you had the privilege of seeing these speakers as an observer in the crowd or live on TV, I bet you have no idea what color ties they had on. It's the power of their messages that has endured. Clothing, like language, always happens somewhere in geographical and social space. [3]

To ensure that the reach of your message remains unshaken, I encourage you to delve into three core pillars of outfit selection before you decide on your next appearance in front of the camera. The **ABC model**, first conceived in this book, sets to establish a frame of reference for your attire.

Audience (A) is determined by who you seek to target with your message. This is, in most cases, a theoretical but hugely significant exercise (unless you have access to detailed demographic data). It acknowledges a set of characteristics, interests, and expectations among your viewers. Which age group and educational level makes up the bulk of your targeted audience? What is the balance between women and men like? Are they clustered in a certain country or region with traditional or liberal attitudes?

Brand (B) comprises what values you intend to project. The step determines a tone for your outfit which often aligns with what you're known for. What do you want viewers to see in you? On an individual level, are you conservative, creative, or rebellious? And when it comes to your industry, whether information technology or finance, how would you characterize it? The answers collectively reflect on your expectations for the dress code to best represent you.

Channel (C) is the network you will appear on. Mark the day of the week and time of the scheduled interview. In this context, you are taking into account how laid back or formal the channel is in terms of the outfits worn by both presenters and guests. Do some additional research and watch some clips of other appearances during the same show and timeslot to refine your fashion compass. Work back week-by-week or day-by-day from when your interview will take place.

Another way to visualize how these three variables powerfully interact is through a classical Venn diagram:

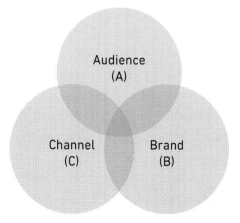

For instance, here's what I've done for my next appearance:

Audience (A) *Professionals looking to get their message out to the world and have people actually listen to what they are trying to get across. These are busy people, anywhere from entry-level consultants to top CEOs, who are deeply frustrated by how difficult communication through television can be. They have strong educational backgrounds and high expectations for quality content. By and large, they handle their personal brands in public well.*

Brand (B) *Yousef Gamal El-Din, cable news anchorman, communication expert, and author. By virtue of the news and finance industry, mostly a man known for conservative, formal attire. Occasionally bold ties put him in a slightly contrarian box within that segment.*

Channel and Time of Broadcast (C) *MSNBC, USA, on Wednesday at 3 PM. Previous guests are mostly laid back with semi-formal wear depending on their respective professions. Tie more of an exception than the rule.*

Outfit Decision: *Dark blue two-piece suit, off-white shirt with cufflinks, and a light blue necktie.*

You may have reached a different conclusion depending on how you defined your ABC fashion variables. Even with the same ABC setup, you may feel a necktie was a bit over the top.

Now it's your turn. Practice by simulating a scheduled appearance on a selection of television programs throughout the week at various times. It can get tricky when you are wearing more than one hat, as in the case of an executive who is also an aspiring art collector. When both the business and the art become part of the conversation, you can creatively weave together elements from each. Run your decision by a friend or the show producer if you are speaking to them directly.

Brand Names and Personal Comfort

It's sensible to wear something you are comfortable in. When a piece of clothing is ill-fitting, it can be so distracting! Although studios are meticulously temperature-controlled, you will still feel the heat from the strong lights. For that reason, wear absorbent fabrics and choose materials that breathe easily.

Equally, make sure the outfit actually fits and is secure. Anything too loose is likely to need adjustment over and over. So, it's always a fine idea to stay with the tried and tested. When you like a piece of clothing a lot, and others tell you that they do too, you feel at ease in it when it's your turn to shine. I've often postponed wearing new clothes on camera as I wanted to get more meaningful feedback from others. Every shred of doubt removed is a token of confidence gained.

What about prominent name brands you ask? They can work if they are congruent with your personal brand, as we see with sports stars like Michael Jordan or Roger Federer. However, if it does not add value to your appearance, its presence will distract. The same applies even for smaller accessories such as badges or name tags when doing interviews at industry conferences.

In the world of comic books, superheroes wear a signature costume that comes to embody their heroism. Superman is a terrific case in point. Who doesn't know Superman? In real life, some individuals also adopt a one-outfit strategy. Steve Jobs was well-known for his tradition of wearing black turtleneck sweaters for public appearances. This readily identifiable outfit conveyed the simplicity trademark he wanted *Apple* to represent. Other one-outfit wonders include famous fashion designers *Carolina Herrera* and *Michael Kors*. Carolina's uniform features a white button-down shirt and a black skirt. As for Michael, it's a black T-Shirt with a black jacket and no socks.

For you, this "signature look" strategy is a risky proposition and has to be considered as the rare exception to the rule. Wearing the same clothes every time you make a camera appearance, especially if it's a frequent occurrence, can create intrigue among viewers unless you have a renowned public profile. Recordings of your appearance will be made available online, and if someone searches you on *YouTube* and watches you wearing the same outfit on five of your recent broadcast moments, you had better have a good reason for it.

Instead, keep a range of TV-ready outfits in rotation. At the beginning of my career, a month would go by without having worn an outfit more than once. I planned it out weeks in advance by keeping a meticulous schedule on a spreadsheet. Eventually, I did cut it down. The truth is that nobody is going to notice whether it's been two or three weeks since you last wore an outfit on your daily appearances.

Outfits for Women

For women, developing a chic television wardrobe isn't quite as simple as it is for their male partner. There are many more options, which can make styling more fun, but these options can also pose a challenge when it comes to figuring out what you're most comfortable in and the look that best supports your message. Plus, women are consistently adapting to shifting cultural norms around workplace attire.

Power dressing, a concept that surfaced in the 1980s "to provide a group of educated, independent women—until then excluded from the male working public sphere—an identity kit to manage the delicate balance between the feminine and the professional"[4] was originally borne of male style conventions. Think pantsuits and shoulder pads. But this has been changing rapidly in recent decades—one only has to look at former First Lady Michelle Obama, TV anchor Megyn Kelly, and the fictional power-hungry Claire Underwood on the TV series *House of Cards* to see that power dressing for today's leading women encompasses a unique blend of the feminine, professional, creative, and chic.

When it comes to Megyn Kelly's fashion choices, the *New York Times* had this to say: "She has become famous for refusing to be boxed in by anyone else's 'appropriate': not her network's, nor a political party's, nor the mythical dos and don'ts of career girl dress."[5] Given her amazing star power, from climbing the ranks at *Fox News* to nabbing her own *NBC* morning show *Megyn Kelly Today*, it's safe to say that defining her own look has in no way hindered her on-camera career, and in fact has further pushed the boundaries for women's fashion on screen.

In Claire Underwood's character, we see a similar reinterpretation of the power dressing style—she is professional, feminine, and in command, "wearing clothes and accessories that are something more than an armour against a male-dominated world."[6] While her outfit choices are far more complex and fashion-forward than her male partner, Francis Underwood, her wardrobe's power statement is arguably stronger.

Given the shifting landscape, I don't provide detailed guidelines for women's outfits in this section. Instead, I share some tips to help you navigate the exciting world of on-camera attire. What you choose to wear for your next appearance will depend on your personal style identity, what you're comfortable in, and the culture of the show or network. Ultimately, the goal for both men and women is always the same: to keep the crowd focused on what is said and not on your wardrobe.

So, do you go with a traditional suit? A nice blouse? A simple dress? First and foremost, consider the fit. Look for pieces that create a pleasing silhouette— clothing that is too loose can make you appear shapeless or sloppy, and clothing that is too tight may subdivide the body and draw too much attention to one area. On the subject of fit, it goes without saying that overly revealing clothing will distract your audience. Be mindful of the cut of your shirt—a scoop neck is a good choice, as it is generally flattering yet modest without being stuffy— as well as the length of your skirt.

When it comes to the length of skirts and dresses, Kristina Moore, founder of *The Corporate Fashionista*, has great advice: "Dresses and skirts that are too short may be a negative distraction for viewers and draw them away from the context of your message. For the best fit length take into consideration age, body type, profession and the TV show's setting. Equally, dresses and skirts that are worn way too long instantly project an ill-fitting and out-of-date image." [7] She also emphasizes the importance of skirt length for seated guest appearances, where you'll need to subtly cross and uncross your legs.

Clean lines are also crucial—avoid a lot of poof, volume, or ruffles, as they can dwarf the body. Tailored dresses and suits complement the body and convey a sense of control and authority. Kristina Moore's go-to is a fitted sheath dress. I go into detail about color in the next chapter; however, a quick tip for women is that jewel tones work well with almost every skin tone. Plus, they can be easily mixed and matched, allowing you to get creative and reuse pieces without repeating entire outfits. Opt for colors that work with your complexion. Additionally, a brightly colored scarf in a complementary color or statement necklace can complete the outfit. It's always best to stick to one statement accessory so your look doesn't get too busy and cluttered.

A Note on Bling

Be sure to be selective about the type and assortment of jewelry you wear. There's a fine line between displaying success and coming across as desperately seeking to make a personal statement.

When choosing jewelry, keep things simple. Jewelry worn close to the face, such as earrings and necklaces, should be minimal and not compete with your facial features. Very large necklaces (or layers of necklaces), oversized rings, bangles, and dangly earrings will be distracting. Also, remember that light reflects off of sparkly objects, so any blinged-out jewelry like watches and rings (this goes for men, too!) can be an issue on camera. You will always do right by your message in choosing tasteful restraint.

That said, jewelry can add lovely contrast to your outfit. Some pieces that work well include plain gold or silver rings, simple chain or pearl necklaces, and statement necklaces with interesting shapes and colored stones.

Outfit Checklist for Women:

- ✓ First, look for a good fit and clean lines.
- ✓ Choose outfits that align with your message.
- ✓ Avoid skirts that are too short or too long.
- ✓ Jewel tones work well with most skin tones.
- ✓ Avoid sparkly accessories.
- ✓ Opt for simple jewelry around the face.

Clothing for Men

In general, a fitted, long-sleeve shirt with a collar, open or buttoned, will go a long way toward keeping you in your comfort zone. Short-sleeves can work in a less formal broadcast setting as established by the outcome of your ABC model.

Test your shirt collar beforehand by ensuring that one or two fingers fit between the collar and your neck when buttoned. A collar that barely fits can restrict your blood circulation in a high-stakes environment such as live programming.

You will want to add a jacket to create sufficient contrast for TV. A buttoned jacket will work even better. If you wear one, make sure it fits well. A jacket that's too big for you will communicate a lack of control to your audience.

To stay cool, put on your jacket just before you step in front of the camera. When you go on-air, pull down your jacket and sit on the back end of it. Any creases in the shoulder area that could make you look hunched forward will be straightened out.

Another technique to enrich contrast is to add a neck or bow tie. Louis XIV, the long-serving French monarch also known as the Sun King, is credited with the first necktie when he wore a *lace cravat* in 1646. Do what comes naturally to you and the brand you represent.

There's no doubt that my upbringing shaped my sense of fashion and nourished a penchant for neckties. A well-tied knot can signal attention-to-detail and balance to viewers.

While there are dozens of ways to tie a necktie, the symmetrical half-Windsor knot impresses and has gotten me a lot of positive feedback over the years. Use a tie clip if you are worried about your tie not staying in place. For taller gentlemen, this is also an excellent workaround for shorter ties.

Wear well-fitted pants and long socks. I've been through several live broadcasts where the guest wore short socks only to give the world a glimpse of their hairy legs. It might work in a beach setting, but in a televised conversation, those legs become the elephant in the room.

I have to also call readers' attention to an emerging nonconformist trend in executive fashion toward bright, colorful socks. I've recently begun experimenting with them myself. Although this may seem stylish for certain occasions, it will be counterproductive on TV as it takes away attention from your face.

You can add an individual expression to your clothing by way of suspenders, or pocket squares, just like the dapper Don Draper in the TV series *Mad Men*.

Elegant cufflinks and a watch are staples of executive fashion that exude prosperity and sophistication. If your hands move on tables a lot, go with a watch that has a leather strap. That way, you won't get any distracting sounds from the strap grinding against the surface of the table.

Finally, to wrap up on your masterful executive appearance, don't forget to polish your shoes.

Outfit Checklist for Men:

✓ Fitted, long-sleeve shirt with a collar.
✓ Add a jacket (and tie) for contrast on TV.
✓ Wear well-fitted pants and long socks.
✓ Stand out with suspenders or pocket squares.
✓ Long socks with colors that match your pants.
✓ Polish your shoes.

Should You Wear Glasses?

I f you wear glasses, and if they've become an integral part of your public persona, then wear them on TV, but get them with lenses that have a clear, anti-reflective coating. With the light passing through to your eyes, this will reinforce eye contact with your listeners. Critical eye contact is addressed separately and is a central focus of *Appearance Routine 4* later in the book.

Anti-glare lenses may occasionally not solve the light reflection problem. In a professional studio with sophisticated lighting equipment, your producer or director can apply additional methods to mitigate the glare from your glasses.

On the other hand, there may be limited lighting flexibility at a remote camera position, and there may not be any network staff on site to assist in calibrating the lights. In such cases, you can try leaning your glasses inward to see if it will reduce the glare. Ask the producer or director speaking to you in your earpiece if glare is still a factor.

Frame style and color can be kept simple so as not to detract from your other facial features. A reliable alternative is to consider contact lenses, provided you are comfortable wearing them. This has been my preference since starting out as an aspiring broadcast journalist.

Given that television's *raison d'*être is to model human-to-human communication, sunglasses are inappropriate even outdoors in harsh sunlight—unless of course you are Jack Nicholson.

Appearance Routine 2

Develop Color Consciousness (C)

C

The notion that color can alter human behavior is captivating. Scientific research has firmly established color as a powerful messenger. But how does our brain interpret color? Does a black suit convey formality or sadness?

The relationship between color and emotion is closely tied to color preferences. In particular, color preferences are associated with whether a color elicits positive or negative feelings. [8]

We do not actively evaluate the colors in people's clothes. Only when they wear something bizarre is our reaction elevated from the subconscious. Even unconscious awareness influences our perceptions, so being armed with color consciousness in front of the camera is a major competitive edge.

In fact, my understanding of color has contributed to some of the most memorable moments on TV. If you keep in mind a few simple cardinal color rules, you'll ensure that your appearance on television will be a resounding success.

To appreciate the potency of color, visualize a spectrum that starts with cool colors, such as purple and the darkest of blues. As the colors become warmer, the index travels through light blue, green, yellow, and orange until it reaches the hot zone of the strongest of reds. The arrangement is based on the wavelength of the individual colors that make up light: the longer the wavelength, the warmer the color.

VISIBLE SPECTRUM

| Red 700 nm | Orange | Yellow | Green | Blue | Indigo | Violet 400 nm |

Beyond red and blue, there are other types of electromagnetic radiation such as ultraviolet (UV) and infrared, but the human eye can't pick those up.

Colors were traditionally considered safe for television when found toward the center of the spectrum. With new camera sensor and digital broadcast technologies, this has largely become a nonissue.

Earth tones are cool, flat colors as they reflect the natural hues found in rocks, dirt, and trees. Examples include beige, brown, gold, burgundy, maroon, and gray. A bit further out on the spectrum you've got pink, mauve, and light blues which are a few other options that work well on TV.

Lighter shades of colors generally make you look younger. As the youngest talent in the network when I first joined *CNBC*, I could not afford to look any younger, so I stayed with darker suits. Medium blue or gray are excellent picks if you're an older gentleman.

My cinnamon brown suit, for example, closely matches my dark brown eyes and hair. You can best tell if an outfit is top notch through the reactions of heartily admiring people you meet.

Green or blue as your base color can be an obstacle if you're working on a virtual set (where a single color in the background is swapped for, say, a busy street in downtown Paris). The color is used for what is called a "chroma key" or green screen. If you wear green (or blue) on a virtual set, those parts of your body will be absorbed by the background picture or video. When unsure about whether there will be a virtual set, ask one of the producers or directors on location.

Hot Colors and Patterns

Bright green, yellow, orange, and especially red are hot in the true sense of the word in that they can cause a bad "bleeding effect" in older camera sensors. The reasons for this fallout are very technical, so let's just say that because I am wearing bright red does not mean that the camera will interpret the color as bright red. I love red neckties, including a lively red Christmas edition that is stunning when worn but underwhelming on television. A compromise I've made is to wear a dark red version that is not as overpowering on camera.

Patterns, whether pinstripes, herringbones, or plaids, often cause problems too. It's a common wardrobe mistake made by both reporters and guests. When you wear something with recurring, fine details it can create a wavy optical illusion known as a shimmer or moiré pattern. The interference is caused by the limited number of horizontal and vertical scan lines in traditional television sets.

Despite the rise of digital broadcasting with high-resolution television, bear in mind that some networks around the world still use less-sophisticated technology. The safe approach is to select patterns that work across the various broadcast platforms. I suggest you stick with solid colors if you would like to err on the side of caution. Patterns can be worn but try them on-camera first.

Combining patterns such as polka dots with stripes is difficult to get right for TV. If you're new to mixing patterns, leave it for another day and keep it simple. Patterns *can* contribute to individual brands, and a case in point is a tie with diagonal stripes to signal business growth.

Black and White

Stark-white shirts or tops tend to dominate the screen and are disruptive. The camera sensor will use your shirt, assuming it is the brightest element, as a base to calibrate other colors, thereby causing those other colors to appear darker. The effect takes away from the brightness of your face.

You may get away with the gleaming white shirt or top if you're wearing a buttoned jacket over it. Still, a softer off-white tone such as light ivory or cream is better.

I had a liking for white, shiny shirts, which is why I did not take this concept to heart for a long time. When I wore a jacket over it, no producers or directors ever called me up to say it was an issue. But I did a few appearances where I had to be less formal (without a jacket), and the plain, white shirt did not work.

"Yousef, do you have any other shirt you can wear? The white one you're wearing is too bright for this shot," I recall the crackling in my earpiece while doing a stand-up to report on unfolding events in the Egyptian capital of Cairo.

Likewise, stay away from pure black outfits. When you decide to come in with a black shirt, the camera sensor will use the darkest black as a base, absorbing the light and details surrounding it. As a result, more light will be required to balance the spectrum, making lighter colors overly white.

Although black can be slimming, it's sometimes too formal for television. Make sure you have the right circumstances before wearing a black outfit. Whether cultural or innate, our reactions to certain hues remain at the center of fierce academic debates. For example, in the West, mourning is linked with the color black, whereas in China, the color of death is white.

If you insist on wearing black, the same mitigating principle applies: add contrast with a tie, jacket, or scarf. People's eyes move to the areas with the highest contrast.

Power Colors

Sounds good, doesn't it? Well the name is justified because this is the color range the matters most. Research has shown that when establishing credibility and trust with an audience, blue is best for both men and women. The calming force of blue is in part due to its ubiquity in nature, from water to the skies.

Darker shades of blue and gray are colors of authority and are common in business outfits. Lighter shades of these same colors are perceived as more neutral and approachable.

On the other hand, red is an assertive and energetic color that demands attention. It's as if you're saying, *"Hey, listen to me. I've got something to say, and you're going to hear it."* Because of its power to stimulate the nervous system, red can be perceived as threatening. It's why the hue is used in warning signs and traffic lights. Furthermore, it makes it not always suitable for executives positioning themselves as conservative managers. Imagine it as a form of audacity.

Here's an exercise: write down five keywords that come to mind when looking at bright red. If the message you are trying to get out to the world is incongruent with those keywords, then a less challenging color is the better choice.

To give you a better sense of how deep some color associations run, the link between red and danger stands out. Academic studies have reconfirmed "the wisdom of using red to communicate danger in systematic signal systems, and suggest that red may be used more broadly in other communication contexts to efficiently convey danger-relevant information." [9]

Note how world leaders, such as former U.S. President Barack Obama and Russian President Vladimir Putin, sport their color combinations. You will see colors of authority as base colors (as in the suit) mixed with cool red or blue neckties for contrast. It may not be as clear-cut as some would like you to believe. Research suggests that "at least in a political setting" wearing a red tie has no effects on judgements. [10]

Pink works great as a tie on a dark suit. I've found pink to resonate positively with my viewers in the past. Researchers surmise that in contrast to red, pink has a calming effect on people.

If you're keen to learn more about the psychology of colors, I recommend grabbing a copy of Joann and Arielle Eckstut's *Secret Language of Color*. It's a time-consuming read but you will find plenty of information there, both current and historical.

Color Consciousness Checklist:

✓ Skip shiny, white shirts. Off-white is better.

✓ Insist on black? Remember to add a little bit of contrast with a tie, jacket, or scarf.

✓ Safe choices for TV: earth tones include cool, flat colors (rocks, dirt, and trees).

✓ Pink, mauve, blues, maroon and burgundy also work well.

✓ Blue is best when establishing credibility and trust with an audience.

✓ Red is an assertive and energetic color.

✓ Dark blues and grays are colors of authority.

Appearance Routine 3

Yes, You Really Need Makeup (M)

M

The fact is that small details are more magnified than ever in the era of high-definition displays and crisp video. Those imperfections can range from dark circles and wrinkles to scars and moles. The evolution of camera lenses will continue unabated in years to come, and it will expose deeper flaws. Under these circumstances, get accustomed to carrying a makeup kit with you if the plan is to go on television.

For the men reading this book, I know what you're going to say. It's the same line I get from the hundreds of executives I've coached: *"Listen, I don't need any makeup,"* they say while glancing awkwardly around the room.

Others laugh out loud and say: *"You're joking, right?"*

The reality is that you *do* need makeup regardless of how you feel about it. Ironically, the process is as effortless or as tedious as you want it to be.

Richard Nixon is said to have lost the first televised U.S. presidential debate against John F. Kennedy in 1960 because he had disregarded the importance of professional makeup. While Kennedy accepted help from a *CBS* makeup artist, Nixon refused, deciding to go instead with a mixture known as "lazy shave" to hide his five o'clock shadow (that is the facial hair growth that occurs after the morning shave). But with the intense, hot lights of the studio, he soon began sweating profusely—with profound consequences.

Chicago Mayor Richard Daley's reported reaction says it all: *"My God, they've embalmed him before he even died."* I encourage you to watch the video made available by the JFK Library online. You can see how desperate and apprehensive Nixon comes across at times. He even pulls out a small handkerchief to dab the sweat away. Can you imagine the extra, nerve-racking pressure of seeing yourself sweat in a situation like that?

It's been decades since that blunder, but makeup debacles are still widespread. The good news is that they are easy to prevent!

The Benefits of Makeup

Makeup helps absorb perspiration and reduces shine, both of which are impediments to a strong TV showing. Glare can also be highlighted by natural oils on your skin that you would normally not notice.

Even small amounts of glare accentuated by powerful studio lights can be a sign of anxiety. If a viewer sees you on television and the studio lights are making you sweat, they may think, *"This person doesn't seem to be certain about the key facts of the argument."* All because of a few tiny sweat pearls or a pale face. It's a high credibility price to pay.

The other awe-inspiring benefit of makeup is its capacity to smooth the skin. It's particularly useful for early-morning television appearances when guests and presenters alike often have breakouts or a shaving rash. The majority of blemishes and smudges fade out with a quick application.

Unfortunately, a lot of guests trust television networks to deliver the luxury of a dedicated makeup artist. Frequently to the dismay of guests, the stylist is busy powdering up someone else. Or the remote camera location you are invited to outside the studio is just that—a remote location. Smaller stations may not even have a makeup artist on call!

Others falsely believe that if they're not assigned a makeup expert before the show, then they can skip the whole process. *"My skin doesn't need makeup ... I'm a TV natural."* It pains me to hear people say that. Take charge of your appearance!

Makeup for Women

As with clothing, the art of applying makeup for women is far more multifaceted than is the case for men. Here are some tips from leading female television presenters and producers.

If possible, put on makeup under lighting conditions similar to those used on-site. First, prepare your skin by applying a moisturizer. Add an oil-free primer to ensure your makeup sticks in place during your appearance.

Foundation is quintessential in makeup for the camera, and as with men, special types of foundation are best for high-definition television (HDTV) since they produce a softer surface that helps reduce visible wrinkles. Use a sponge or brush to work the foundation onto your skin. When correctly applied, the thin coating will give your face a natural base.

You also have the options of using airbrush and spray foundations. While they may last longer than traditional makeup, they are time-consuming to set up.

Consider a concealer if you have deep circles under your eyes. You want to be fresh for the camera. That is easier said than done, especially if the filming is taking place in the early hours of the morning!

Now apply a white powder to oily areas like your T-zone. The challenge with alternatives like translucent powders is that they contain silica, a light-reflecting ingredient. *MAKE UP FOR EVER's HD Microfinish Powder* is made for HDTV but can still let you down when facing flash photography where light can reflect off certain portions of your face, causing a "flash back."

Television appearances are neither the time or place to experiment with brash makeup colors. Instead, classic looks create that soft, polished presence that is elegant under the strong television lights.

Avoid heavy eye shadows, and go for neutral colors such as gray, as well as some mascara. You can experiment with a touch of makeup highlighter under the eyebrows for additional definition. Brush and line the eyebrows into a soft arch to perfect them. Stray hairs will stand out.

On your lips, as with your eyes, less is again better. Steer clear of dark matte lip colors. Opt instead for a soft pink or red. To create a wider coverage, use a lip brush to apply the color. For the final touch, add a layer of sheer gloss.

Makeup Checklist for Women:

✓ Classic looks create that soft, polished presence that is elegant under strong lights.

✓ Add an oil-free primer to keep your makeup in place during your appearance.

✓ Special types of foundation for HDTV produce a softer surface that reduces visible wrinkles.

✓ Consider a concealer if you have deep circles under your eyes. Apply a powder to oily areas.

✓ Avoid heavy eye shadows, and go for neutral colors such as gray, plus some mascara.

✓ For lips, use soft pink or red.

✓ Add a layer of sheer gloss.

What Works for Men?

Now that we've established the need for makeup for a professional television appearance, you will need to acquire the right kit. In the broadcast world, men use powder-foundation combinations, such as *MAC's Studio Fix Powder Plus Foundation*, to create a matte and smooth finish. These products are also handy due to their small size. If you go to a makeup store, they will match your skin tone with the precise shade.

As you select a makeup kit, buy a small brush to use instead of the sponge that comes with the powder. The brush will allow for a more blended application of the makeup.

Makeup will also lighten the five o'clock shadow, which can look atrocious on camera. I usually razor shave at least eight hours before a live appearance. The time you need to shave will of course vary depending on how quickly your facial hair grows.

When applying makeup, aim for subtlety — and less is better — for too much makeup would be dreadful on screen. At the very least, powder your nose, forehead, and face as to not appear shiny. If you are bald or balding, extend the coverage to the edge of your receding hairline.

Also add a bit of natural lip balm for a polished, healthy presence. *Burt's Bees* and *Labello* have served me well over the years.

Most television news networks have an unspoken rule when it comes to facial hair. The clean, close shave is the *modus operandi*. Sure, you've got your exceptions, like my former colleague Jim Cramer. Guests have understandably more bandwidth to experiment, but as with clothing, television is an opportunity to project your brand.

I'll never forget the day when *CNBC* had invited a political analyst on set. His hair was all over the place, and he had a long, unkempt beard. To this day, I'm not sure what look he was going for. Although many of us found him entertaining at the time, nobody was listening to what he was saying. The story serves as another testament to never obscure your message by your appearance.

Makeup Checklist for Men:

✓ Use powder-foundation combos, such as *MAC's Studio Fix,* for a smooth finish.
✓ Go for a brush instead of a sponge.
✓ Razor shave at least eight hours before an appearance to steer clear of skin irritations.
✓ Powder your nose, forehead, and face.
✓ Add a bit of natural lip balm.

Keep It Clean

Here's a tip I learned the hard way: get into the habit of having your own makeup brush. Just like other grooming products, it's better they not be shared with others since they can transfer skin bacteria and cause infections.

When you are finished with your television program, you can remove the makeup with special cleansing wipes or lotion. Both are widely available and take off everything in a couple of strokes. It ensures your pores remain unclogged and prevents your face from becoming a breeding ground for future skin breakouts.

Some of these products can leave your facial skin dry, so if you're in front of the camera for long periods, you may want to consider picking up a moisturizing cream.

If you want to get serious about makeup on camera, consult Hollywood makeup artists Gretchen Davis and Mindy Hall's *The Makeup Artist Handbook* for a comprehensive visual guide to professional techniques.

Capitalize on Body Language (B)

B

You've by now adopted several appearance routines, and you're already making awesome progress toward credible self-expression.

Well done! Still, we have two more routines you can leverage to captivate your audience.

Just like in other situations in your life when you're aiming to mesmerize a person, getting the body language right is a pivotal ingredient of a potent appearance cocktail. The structured reality of TV blossoms when we act naturally. A cascade of academic studies has shown that nonverbal communication trumps the spoken word in importance by a significant margin. Unfortunately, there's no mathematical equation for it. But together with my experience and existing scientific literature, we can outline in this chapter how to get your body language to support your overall camera appearance. It's all about alignment, as we did with clothing, colors, and makeup.

The art of standing in front of the camera demands authoritative simplicity, akin to the 20 percent effort that yields 80 percent of results. Contrary to what a substantial portion of self-help literature suggests, you don't need to be a body language magician to leverage its select powers. That's our benchmark.

Stand Up

For a start, it's more advantageous to stand than to sit. Being on your feet puts you in a naturally alert frame of mind. I take standing over sitting any day because it automatically gives me a consistent energy boost right off the starting blocks. Too bad—it's not always a choice. You will be sitting for the most part in the studio and standing at remote camera locations.

Stand Still

When you are standing, stay grounded rather than move around with your legs or sway. The camera is in a fixed position, and since you are not performing for *Dancing with the Stars,* moving from your spot, even a little shift, can push you out of the frame. Although it may be obvious, it's easy to forget once you are in front of the camera and in your element!

Let's assume you are invited by a leading news network to comment on the British election results from a position outside the Houses of Parliament in London. To be most effective, you can stand in one of two ways: either have one foot slightly forward or have your feet apart horizontally by about 40 centimeters (16 inches), depending on how tall you are.

The key here is to find a *comfortable* position. Give both of these options a try, and stick with the position that allows you to focus on the message. One way or the other, you will give the image of someone who's in control.

Sit Tall

In the course of interviewing leading executives, I've seen how they either lie back in a crouch or sit up awkwardly straight. Both impair your trustworthiness and are likely to create erroneous perceptions with your audience. Sit overly relaxed, and viewers will gather you are not taking the conversation seriously. Sit excessively straight, and viewers will see a person who is uptight or on edge.

The *right compromise* is to sit straight and lean forward by 10-20 degrees. This posture makes you look slimmer and relatable. The result: you appear engaged and comfortable. Watch out for swivel chairs. Turning left and right will not give a positive impression on screen and can even be interpreted as showing "negative feelings toward the person one is talking to." [11]

Meanwhile, high armchairs can push your shoulders upward in what will look like a shrug. While unintended, the posture comes across as submissive and apologetic to your audience. My longer arms make this a continuous struggle!

Mind Your Legs

One leg crossed over the other can communicate defensiveness, but it is popular with decision-makers because it implies a sense of wisdom. At least 80 percent of the men and women I have interviewed favor this position.

As a kid, I would see my father, a corporate lawyer, sitting in a crossed-leg position when I was able to visit him at the office. I've incorporated that position to a certain extent, finding it comfortable. Alternatively, I also find myself at times with both feet on the ground for a more neutral, assertive stance.

Use caution, however, when crossing one ankle over the knee for it lays bare the sole of your shoe. It's an inappropriate gesture in some parts of the world.

Show You're Listening

We human beings tend to put our hands in our pockets or cross our arms over our body instinctively when we are uncomfortable. Here's the signal you're sending: *"I lack confidence and I'm bored."* It's tempting to fall back into your comfort zone, especially in a new environment, which is why you have to remind yourself of these points ahead of an interview.

A number of trainees ask me what they're supposed to do with their arms and hands. *"I can't just… well sit there and do nothing!"* a managing director of an established emerging market investment fund once confided.

"Do what you would normally do," was the simple answer he did not see coming. *"I'm certain you don't put them behind your back and clasp them together when you are chatting with a potential client, colleague, or even a friend."*

Allow your hands to move freely as long as they're on a level not higher than your shoulders. If you raise them higher, you will be interfering with the camera shot of your face.

The message here is not to worry about your arms or hands. This allows innate human communication to then take its course.

If your hands tend to fret, give them something to do that can add value. A pen, for example, can infuse an element of wisdom. It's a bit harder to stop feet fidgeting!

Camera operators and producers love people who are natural because it's what people want to see and can best associate with. They may even film a "cut-away" and show a close-up of your hand motion. These additional visuals allow the audience to better interpret the setting.

Clenched fists, as an illustration, would help in a story about a person whose home was foreclosed or an athlete showing anger at an opponent for foul play.

For the same reason, nod your head when somebody else is speaking or inject acknowledgments to demonstrate that you're listening.

As you go about your camera appearance, resist the urge to fix your hair, touch your nose, or cover your mouth when nervous. Such anxiety-ridden reflexes are tied to your subconscious limbic system and can be difficult to reign in.

For a detailed exploration of body language, look up Joe Navarro's *What Everybody is Saying*.

What Smile is Appropriate?

The smile is a key factor in the way humans interact, particularly on a video platform where conscious as well as subconscious visual perceptions come into play. It's a typical example of what scholars refer to as nonverbal cues.

We grow up with adages such as *"smile for the camera,"* or *"say cheese,"* but nobody ever tells you to what extent you're supposed to smile. Do you show your teeth a little? Is it better to just smile as much as possible? Do you display a full-size grin to convey joy?

The rise of online messaging has upset our internal compass for nonverbal cues. When texting on your favorite platform, whether on the go or in the office, you have a palette of standardized emojis. They have served to trivialize the striking nuances of human communication.

You can easily practice smiling using the camera on your mobile phone and the gracious time of a friend or colleague. Get them to tell you a funny story that happened to them today, and let them record you during the exercise. A couple of minutes later, take a separate video and capture a few on-demand camera smiles. Then compare the two clips. Before long, you will begin to get a deeper sense for what is natural.

It took me a while to find my own balance because I developed the habit as a youngster of flashing my teeth to convey agreement, joy, or when around a camera. *"Let's see that grin!"* I remember our high school photographer cheering from behind the camera. Professional photographers will crack a joke instead to make you laugh naturally.

Why do we care? Because on-demand smiles, as you probably experienced for yourself in the exercise, are easy to spot. In a natural smile or laugh, the cheeks are fully lifted by the two muscles around the eyes, a reflex that produces what is called "crow's feet." A fake smile, on the other hand uses one muscle only.

Although there appears to be a consensus around the benefits of smiling more, it depends once again on your message and audience. A broad smile might be useful when "warmth or friendliness is the focus (e.g. on *Facebook*), but moderation is recommended when signals of competence are the primary goal (e.g. on *LinkedIn*)." [12]

In the structured world of broadcast, what facial expression should you adopt as your baseline throughout the program? The soft smile is your starting point, with your mouth closed as a gesture of confidence.

What we are looking for on television is a hint of a smile to let viewers know that you are in charge.

Practice the baseline smile with your camera phone. It's from that point that you move forward depending on the subject at hand. If a hurricane is about to hit the East Coast in the United States, then you can reduce the baseline smile to form a neutral expression.

You'll ask: *"Should I not look really sad or concerned? It's a hurricane for crying out loud!"* Television has you covered in that the transmission mechanism will dampen your expression. It's akin to a small part lost in translation.

The camera magnifies minor variations, including nonverbal cues like smiles. All you are doing is flowing with the way the medium functions.

Also, imagine folks on camera who keep their mouth open or produce a sudden grin that has nothing to do with the topic on hand. What is your first reaction? Facial expressions like that are associated with artificiality and are counterintuitive to a credible appearance.

How to Handle Eye Contact

Our eyes are powerful communicators of our emotions. After all, they've been romanticized throughout history as the window to the soul. That is, in part, why eye contact is a challenge newcomers to the camera world find overwhelming. Even seasoned commentators still make mistakes on this one.

Understanding how eye contact works in front of the camera is critical because it can make or break any connection you're seeking to secure with your audience. The attention span of the average viewer is a diminishing commodity. If you miss the opportunity to connect, the viewer might change the channel, and the next two minutes of your well-prepared messaging points will never get through. I've fortunately put together some basic guidelines for eye contact on camera.

Firstly, if you're in the studio, confirm with the presenter where they want you to look. You'll be looking at the presenter in most cases, although there can be situations with remote studio guests where you're supposed to direct your eyes toward them. You should be given guidance as to which camera to look into when speaking or listening to guests.

If your lines of sight are not set *a priori*, you'll end up confused and peeking around the studio in search of help in the form of a signal or gesture. The audience will all the while interpret your glances around the room as a signal of evasiveness. They cannot perceive that you're only trying to find out where to look!

Darting glances come off as untrustworthy. In our day-to-day interactions with other people, it is normal to regularly break eye contact as it otherwise may be perceived as threatening. It's a different story, once again, in television.

Maintain eye contact if you're talking to the camera or presenter. If you keep breaking eye contact, you'll give the impression that you're trying to hide something. It's a reaction that also happens as a result of sheer anxiety. If you need to look away from the camera or presenter, pick something close by to focus on briefly to collect your thoughts, and then look back at the camera or presenter.

This approach helps us steer clear of sweeping movements, say in the direction of the ceiling or the floor, both of which will erode the strength of the TV appearance. Who wants to be a deer in the headlights?

Not using "shifty eyes" is not the same as freezing your eyes. Just be yourself. Your eyes will subtly turn in different directions depending on the commentary you are crafting and what areas of your brain these are tapping. Looking to the left for example is an indicator of visual thought, such as recalling the color of a flower.

There are still pockets in the broadcast industry that are obsessed with maximizing eye contact when it comes to presenters, although research as far back as the 1980s suggests delivering a monologue is perceived as less compelling when compared to working with a script. [13]

As we did earlier with practicing the smile, use your camera phone to record yourself discussing a random subject for two minutes. Then watch it while the clip is on mute, carefully observing your eyes. The camera lens is devoid of any human expressions we can relate to. It can be hard at the beginning to truly emulate the way you would speak as if there was a real person in front of you.

With that said, don't forget to blink as you would in any given chat. A cold stare can be unsettling for anybody. Do your best not to blink too much either since that might indicate stress. Your "blink rate" is an unconscious process that adapts automatically to different conditions. If you're thinking about it now, it's best not think about it!

One more tip: bright lights are integral components of a television studio. You will be squinting at the beginning as your eyes adjust to the new lighting environment. If after a few moments you are still uncomfortable, or if your eyes are sensitive to the bright lights, talk to the producer or director to see whether a minor adjustment can be made. It is your prerogative as a guest to be comfortable, and your reputation is at stake. The act of squinting disturbs the precious eye contact viewers seek to make.

Build Your
Confidence (C)

n this chapter, I will showcase physical and mental tricks of the trade to empower you with on-camera gravitas. A set of easy-to-adopt, short exercises will immediately assuage your anxiety and boost your confidence shortly before it's go-time. It's a way of controlling the butterflies in your stomach. Remember, a little anxiety serves you well, for it gives you an energy kick when you're under the spotlight.

Your on-camera show is an exercise just like with any other physical activity, so we've got to warm up!

Have you ever heard of a short-distance sprinter, such as Usain Bolt, going straight for the dash without first loosening up? That is what a camera appearance feels like thanks to the inevitable adrenaline rush. A typical warm-up for a sprinter can last up to one hour. The good news is that your warm-up need not take that long!

Relax

Begin by loosening your shoulders and rolling them downward, for when we are tense, we tend to pull our shoulders up. Shake out your arms while fully extended. Then stretch your neck slowly upward, and take a few deep breaths to ensure your lungs are primed. Oxygen consumption will be higher while on-air.

If you have done yoga or meditation, you will be familiar with a few breathing techniques. Be conscious of how you're inhaling and exhaling as it is essential for effective voice projection. Let's start with diaphragm breathing.

Stand with your feet comfortably apart. Loosen your stomach, place your hand on your belly, and then breathe in slowly through your nose so that your stomach is pushed out. That would be your diaphragm rising. Count to four and then breathe out through your mouth. Repeat the drill twice.

Loosen Your Tongue

I do a few smile stretches (that's my own creative jargon) and tongue twisters to avoid stumbling over words. It's quite commonplace in our industry, although not everyone will admit to it. The smile stretch is just a full smile, holding it for four seconds and then repeating the exercise two times. Bonus benefit: just flashing a smile feeds positive energy.

Let's get your tongue warmed up. Over-enunciate the following words when you say them, and increase your speed with every repetition. Here are a couple of tongue twisters that followed me throughout my live television career:

She sells seashells by the seashore
The shells she sells are surely seashells
So if she sells shells on the seashore,
I'm sure she sells seashore shells

Peter Prangle the prickly pear picker
picked three pecks of prickly pears
from the prickly pear trees
on the pleasant prairies

Hum loudly for 15 seconds. This loosens up your lips and facial muscles. Begin with lips relaxed and gently closed and then slide your voice from a high to a low pitch.

And now for a run-through of some vowels:

'A' for ahhhh and 'E' is eeeeeeee,
'I' is iiiii 'O' is oooooo and 'U' is uuuuuu

It's advisable not to do these exercises when you're on a busy train or bus on your way to the studio. But once in the office, it's all game for me. I like to bring it all together with one of the more famous songs of Elvis Presley.

Do these before you head out in the morning. You have other options as well such as practicing during a short walk, in the car, in the elevator, or while you are waiting at the television station — not to mention in the shower.

The Energy to Go Live

The task of being in front of the camera can be hugely taxing, and you need to be prepared for it both psychologically and physically.

Leading personalities I interview are frequently surprised by how much energy is burned by going on-camera. Here is a comment I recall from the CEO of one of the largest oil and gas companies in the world after we had gone off-air:

"That was exhausting, Yousef," he said, as he collected his papers from the studio desk. *"How long were we on-air for? Ten minutes?"*

"A little bit over three minutes, actually," I replied. He was astonished.

The stress of the situation caused time to unfold slowly for him, and fatigue then set in as the adrenaline rush faded.

In this day and age, audiences feature shorter attention spans with higher expectations for content. Energy for your presentation is crucial for keeping them engaged and entertained. When you speak into a camera, some of the energy gets lost in the process. That's why you have to be louder and clearer than when you're in other situations. It may strike you as embarrassing at first, but you'll get used to it.

To fully create the energy in earlier years, I used to drink two to three cups of coffee before going on the studio set. However, the problem becomes tolerance (as with the majority of stimulants). Recently, I've managed to recalibrate toward just one cup of tea to better *control* the energy.

The presentation style of business networks like *Bloomberg Television* and *CNBC* is faster than other channels such as *CNN* or *Sky News*. Like *really fast*. Combine that with the need to simultaneously monitor several live data screens and listen to various producers and directors providing guidance regarding coverage plans for the next minute or two (through your earpiece, no less), and you begin to get an idea of the energy that's needed. We haven't even begun talking about breaking news!

Part of the pressure comes from the fact that you need to deliver your top performance in a very specific amount of time. It's not like you can choose when to deliver it. If you're going to be live at say 8:36 AM for two minutes, you have to make it happen. It's all about managing **top state**, the highest energy condition of mind and body for a given camera appearance. The concept is in principle a derivative from the widely known peak state.

It's comparable to a tennis player in the final game at Wimbledon. The match gets underway at a set time, and it's a high-stress situation, to say the least. If you're not physically and mentally ready, you'll lose out to your cutthroat competition. And readiness is a byproduct of training.

If your TV appearance is not live, then you've got a bit of leeway. The relief will only be temporary, for once the camera starts rolling, the pressure to perform (and to deliver that optimal performance) gets relentless again. The perception that a recorded interview is easier than a live one is overhyped.

Here is what you can do to achieve confidence, enthusiasm, and control in front of the camera.

Manage your caffeine dose wisely. Up your caffeine intake to one notch above your usual daily consumption. You can indulge in a cup of tea or coffee before you go on. Your response to the caffeine may vary depending on whether you have been a regular consumer of copious caffeine amounts in the past. So, if you usually do not drink coffee, a sudden caffeine surge with say two shots of espresso can cause jitters and anxiety.

Note: when you consume two to three cups of coffee in four or five hours, like I used to do, the slowdown is going to be more pronounced later in the day. The half-life of caffeine in adults is up to six hours!

Apart from the health benefits of occasional intake, tea has a fascinating amino acid known as l-theanine. It balances out the caffeine lift a notch—the behavioral outcome is one where you feel less on edge.

It's best to avoid dairy-based products (milk, cheese, and so on) or syrupy drinks shortly before stepping in front of the camera. These increase the production of phlegm in your throat and diminish the clarity of your voice. Instead of focusing on what you are going to say, you'll be busy clearing your throat.

As in any industry where sharpness of mind is required, I've met people who use drugs to spike their television readiness, including lower-tier prescription stimulants such as *Adderall* and *Provigil* (also known as *Modafinil*). These, however, backfire rapidly. Our journey is about creating sustainable, consistent appearances on TV. That is how you build a true rapport with your audience.

If you appear regularly on television or in front of an audience, and you strongly feel that mental acuity is lagging, you can experiment with herbal supplements such as bacopa and rhodiola.

The last source of potential positive energy comes from passionate content. Make it a habit to jot down three to four core points you will get across to your viewers, even if they constitute only a few key words. The best messages are those that resonate deeply with not just with your target audience but you as well. You can uncover words and expressions you would normally not be able to find when over-scripting in preparation. What exactly is it about the subject that you find amazing? Effective television messaging can be discussed in much more detail and is the subject of another book.

Create Momentum Naturally

When you're on top of your appearance game, not only do you extend the reach of your message, but you also mature into a personality who viewers want to be around. To achieve top state, your mind and body will require the right nutrients at regular intervals.

The benefit of striving for top state in front of the camera lens is that it will extend into day-to-day health benefits. Your energy reserves will increase considerably.

Nutrition is but half the story. When was the last time you worked out? Build regular exercise into your schedule. It will enhance your natural energy flow by getting your "happy hormones" moving. These chemicals, the best-known of which include dopamine, serotonin, oxytocin, and endorphin, can do wonders for your confidence. With extra activity, your sluggishness will begin to dissipate. Your energy will go a notch higher within days of regular training, and every bit of energy won will improve your television appearances.

I currently go for a daily two-mile power walk and circuit training at the gym with tennis three times a week. Unlike swimming, walking and running are great for multitasking as well: you can listen to a podcast or tie up a few phone calls. You don't need a one-hour power sweat session to gain energy. Just get rolling.

Lastly, stress. Exercise is a convenient antidote to stress, for mental activity puts you in the present mindset, leaving behind lamenting over the past or feeling anxious about the uncertainties of the future. Stress depletes your energy and provides for a sluggish television appearance. If you cannot handle stress at the office, do not bring it with you to the studio, let alone to your viewers. It's a privilege to be on TV. The camera lens will magnify the negative energy expressed through your body language.

NUTRIENT RECOMMENDATIONS FOR GOING ON CAMERA

1. **Stay hydrated** with enough water to keep your energy reservoir intact and maintain the optimal body temperature. Our bodies contain roughly 70 percent water!
2. **Fruit** is an excellent source of healthy carbohydrates, vitamins, and minerals. Go with those in the lower range of the glycemic index to prevent spikes in your blood sugar. Those include apples, oranges, grapefruits, strawberries, and cherries.
3. Fresh **green vegetable juice** swiftly alkalizes your cells. I got into an obsession of creating smoothies, including everything from cucumbers to celery.

A word of caution on numbers 4 and 5:
may cause allergic reactions for those with food allergies.

4. **Unsalted, raw nuts** nourish your body with high-energy nutrients.
5. Half a teaspoon of **honey** is about three to four grams of healthy carbohydrates content. You can also sprinkle in some cinnamon for an added lift! An alternative to honey for those on a low-carb diet is a spoon of coconut oil.

Review and Seek Feedback

I f you are still uncertain about which way to go with your appearance, try one more time to get a feel for the program you'll be taking part in. Watch some episodes with an eye on what the presenters were wearing and make a note of what you liked or disliked.

Also, passionate producers love to have a say in what their guests wear, so give them a call and see what they think. At the very least, they can help you make up your mind if you're unsure about a couple of outfit options.

That doesn't mean having bags stacked with clothing from five fashion stores and running up to the producer forty-five minutes before the show to ask which one looks better. You would make yourself and everybody around you nervous.

Relying only on recommendations from producers or presenters is nevertheless dicey at best. They are fallible and do not always care about you showing up at your absolute best. The newsroom is an intensely busy place on an ordinary day. When a big story breaks, it morphs into a beehive of activity.

Cable networks are under immense pressure to cut costs, and fashion specialists will likely be in short supply. It's a common misconception that all news anchors and contributors have a stylist. That is why the skills addressed in this book are indispensable to your public appearance strategy.

Another clothing option within your reach comes in handy when the unpredictable strikes. In the randomness of life's moments, it could be a spilled cup of coffee, or a drop of tomato sauce from a plate of pasta during lunch. Both have happened to me before and it wasn't even my fault! The spare shirt can save your reputation when the stakes are as high as they are on live television.

When you're done, watch a recording of yourself to gauge how your outfit worked out. You can then fine-tune for future appearances.

With my height at six feet six, and square shoulders, a trip to the tailor is like an adventure into the wilderness. Earlier in my career, I would wear jackets with regular shoulder pads that made my shoulders slightly bigger than they needed to be. Later, I would embrace a more natural shoulder design, reducing the padding by at least two-thirds. My journey to recapture appearance proportionality would probably have been delayed for a few more years had it not been for regular feedback from friends and experts.

It's Showtime

The final countdown is about to begin. A member of staff has come to usher you to the studio for the long-awaited moment of truth. You are perfectly placed for a strong showing after having read this book.

Before you go, check that there is nothing in your teeth or on the front or back of your clothing. Brush your lapels and shoulders to remove any hair or dust. A compact lint roller can do this effectively. Once you are in the studio, take a look at yourself on a monitor to resolve issues that may pose problems. It's the only way to get an idea of what you'll look like on video. For instance, the cable of the microphone could be dangling depending how it was placed. If you have a question or concern, approach the presenter directly at this point. Every second counts! Always, always take charge of your appearance.

One way of making last-minute changes is by adjusting your distance to the camera. You might have heard that the camera adds a few pounds. Unfortunately, (or fortunately, depending on your weight anxieties) that is true. The closer you are to the camera the weightier you'll appear.

Don't beat yourself up during the interview. By questioning your performance during the performance, you'd be creating a vicious circle of self-doubt. You'll stumble, draw blanks, and begin showing the staple, nonverbal signs of anxiety we discussed earlier. Mistakes are what make us human. Enjoy the moment, and don't overthink it. Be yourself.

Reignite the positive energy that is in you. Remind yourself: ***"My word carries a lot of weight. That is why I am about to be on television. And I will deliver my message passionately."***

Finally, keep a glass of room temperature water easily accessible. You never know when you might need it. The same goes for your makeup to displace any shininess on your face during commercial breaks.

With these simple exercises, you'll be ready to inspire the people who have tuned in to hear what you have to say.

If there is one thought I'm keen to leave with you after thousands of hours of live television: keep it simple. There is no perfect camera appearance. That's why it's an art (with scientific elements). My big hope and desire is that the five **OC-M-BC** appearance routines become cornerstones of your personal and professional life. You don't have to be a movie superstar anymore for the cameras to come and find you. There are cameras everywhere!

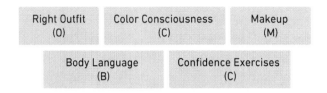

| Right Outfit (O) | Color Consciousness (C) | Makeup (M) |
| Body Language (B) | Confidence Exercises (C) | |

Practice is at the heart of each appearance routine we addressed. Watch yourself on video with the sound turned down to get a better sense of your outfit and body language.

Input from friends and colleagues will help as well. If you see something that either works well or turns out not as impressive as you had thought, make a note of it for next time. The path to your best looks on camera will always be a work-in-progress.

Your audience sees people on television all the time. Not many of them raise the volume to listen. You now have the building blocks in place to make sure they do.

Over time, and with this book serving as a trustworthy guide, you'll be able to acquire a feel for the most appropriate appearance for each on-camera appearance, whether for a press conference or when moderating a live panel discussion.

You've eliminated the mental constraints and intimidating barriers to make a great impression on camera. Let the principles I've outlined help you cultivate a skill set for exciting results.

And as you keep developing these routines, you'll create a camera profile that is uniquely you and highly potent as a messaging platform. With this concise training, the requests for you to appear on camera will flourish.

On a parting note, I would love to hear your feedback. Do share with me what your experience has been like in front of the camera.

You can reach me through social media or directly via yousef@executiveappearance.com.

I look forward to seeing you shine on screen!

Cheat Sheet

---

23 Quick Tips for TV Success

Are you just about to go on-air? Looking for a quick, compact guide to refresh your memory and take charge of your appearance? We've put together twenty-three razor-sharp tips you absolutely can't ignore before going on camera. And it will take you less than ten minutes to review!

1. Don't distract the viewer with your outfit.

2. Dress comfortably. Stay with tried and tested.

3. Shiny, white shirts are disruptive.
    Off-white is better.

4. Add contrast with a tie, jacket, or scarf.

5. Safe choices for TV: earth tones include
    cool, flat colors (rocks, dirt, and trees).
    Pink, mauve, blues, maroon and burgundy
    also work well.

6. Combining patterns such as polka dots with
    stripes is difficult to get right. Keep it simple.

7. Blue is best when establishing credibility. Dark blues and grays are colors of authority. Red is an assertive color.

8. Don't rely on the makeup artist. Smaller stations may not even have one on call.

9. When applying makeup, aim for subtlety— less is better. TV is not the place to experiment.

10. Find a comfortable position. If seated, sit straight and lean forward by 10–20 degrees.

11. Hands out of pockets. Relax. Allow your hands to move freely as long as they're not higher than your shoulders.

12. Use a soft smile with your mouth closed as your baseline. We're looking for a hint of a smile to let viewers know you're in charge.

13. Confirm with network staff where to look during the interview. Nod your head when somebody else is speaking or inject acknowledgments.

14. Bright lights are common in a studio. If you are uncomfortable, talk to the producer.

15. Maintain eye contact. If you need to look away, pick something close by to focus to collect your thoughts, and then look back at the camera or presenter.

16. Do a tongue twister to avoid stumbling over words. Run through vowels and hum loudly for a minute.

17. You have to be louder and clearer. Energy is crucial for keeping an audience engaged.

18. Caffeine boost. Get one if you need it.

19. Hold off on dairy products or syrupy drinks before your interview. Go for a piece of fruit and stay hydrated.

20. If possible, take a look at yourself on the monitor to resolve issues.

21. A last review. Check that there's nothing in your teeth or on your clothing.

22. Keep a glass of water and makeup accessible for commercial breaks.

23. There is no reason to beat yourself up during the interview. Enjoy the moment, and don't overthink it.

About the Author

Yousef Gamal El-Din is a news anchor, bestselling author and entrepreneur.

With many years as the creator and face of top-rated international programs, he has developed cutting-edge strategic counsel on how to shape one's image for maximum clout on TV and on stage.

In over a decade of live television, Gamal El-Din has hosted high-profile figures including heads of state, CEOs and billionaires. He joined *Bloomberg TV* in 2016 after five years as an anchor with *CNBC* in London.

As a regional correspondent, Gamal El-Din courageously reported from hotspots across the Arab World at defining historical moments. It was at Egyptian Television where his career began as a young broadcaster.

He graduated with two journalism degrees from the American University in Cairo, and is fluent in four languages. Although a hardcore globetrotter, home bells ring in Cairo and Zurich.

www.yousefgamaleldin.com

Acknowledgments

There are a lot of people that played a role in making this book come together. I have been lucky in that their support has always been unwavering.

A heartfelt thanks to my editors, who gave me thoughtful guidance throughout the writing process. My gratitude also goes to my friends, including Dalya Katoah, Tassos Pantziarides and Lubna Bouza, who read various stages of the book and offered me candid feedback.

My deepest thanks go to my family who have been wonderful. My parents, Helene and Amin, for encouraging me from a young age to explore the beauty of languages and my Swiss-Egyptian heritage. My brother, Karam, whose strengths have always been my weaknesses. And, of course, my uncle, Hussein Amin, for helping me discover my talent for the television camera.

Finally, wherever we've met: Thank you for your presence and for making an impact.

Notes

1   A. Cauwenberge, G. Schaap, & R. Van Roy, (2014), Effects
    of second-screen viewing and task relevance on cognitive
    load and learning from news, *Computers in Human Behavior*,
    100–109.

2   NASA. (2018, February 12), From John F. Kennedy Moon
    Speech—Rice Stadium, er.jsc.nasa.gov/seh/ ricetalk.htm.

3   J. Faiers & M. Bulgaralla, (2016), *Colors in fashion*.
    New York: Bloomsbury Publishing.

4   R. Ando, R., (2015, December), Fashion and fandom
    on TV and social media: Claire Underwood's power
    dressing. *Critical Studies in Fashion & Beauty*, 6(2), 207-231.
    www.doi.org/10.1386/csfb.6.2.207_1

5   Vanessa Friedman, (2016, December 17), "No one tells
    Megyn Kelly what to wear," *New York Times.*

6   R. Ando, (2015, December), Fashion and fandom on TV
    and social media: Claire Underwood's power dressing.
    Critical Studies in Fashion & Beauty, 6(2), 207-231. www.doi.org/
    10.1386/csfb.6.2.207_1

7   Kristina Moore, (2010, February 21), "What to wear: On
    TV—5 tips to looking great," *Corporate Fashionista.*

8   N. Kaya, & H. Epps, (2004), Relationship between color and emotion: A study of college students. *College Student Journal.*

9   A. Elliot, K, Pravossoudovitch, F. Cury, & S. Young, (2014), Is red the colour of danger? Testing an implicit red–danger association. *Ergonomics*, 503-510.

10 R. Kramer, (2016), The red power(less) tie. *Evolutionary Psychology*, 14.

11 D. Mortensen, (2011), *Communication Theory*. New York: Transaction Publishers.

12 Z. Wang, H. Mao, Y. Li, & F. Liu, (2017), Smile big or not? Effects of smile intensity on perceptions of warmth and competence. *Journal of Consumer Research*, 787–805.

13 B. Gunter, (1987), *Poor reception: Misunderstanding and forgetting broadcast news*. New York: Routledge.

Made in the USA
Middletown, DE
26 July 2021